6-13-07

X

The
Miracle
of Water

The
Miracle
of Water

Masaru Emoto

ATRIA BOOKS
New York London Toronto Sydney

BEYOND WORDS
PUBLISHING

ATRIA BOOKS
1230 Avenue of the Americas
New York, N.Y. 10020

20827 N.W. Cornell Road, Suite 500
Hillsboro, Oregon 97124-9808
503-531-8700 tel
503-531-8773 fax
www.beyondword.com

English translation by David A. Thayne

Originally published as "Jibun ga Kawaru Mizu no Kiseki" by Masaru
Emoto. Copyright © 2007 by I.H.M. Co., Ltd. Water-crystal photography
© 2007 by I.H.M., Co., Ltd.

The information contained in this book is intended to be educational.
The author and publisher are in no way liable for any misuse of
the material.

Library of Congress Catologing-in-Publication Data
Emoto, Masaru, 1943–
    [Jibun ga kawaru mizu no kiseki. English]
    The miracle of water / by Masaru Emoto ; [English translation by
David A. Thayne]. — 1st Atria Books/Beyond Words hardcover ed.
      p. cm.
    1. Water—Health aspects.   2. Water—Philosophy.   3. Conduct of
life. I. Title.
RA591.5.E4513   2007
613.2′87—dc22

                             2006029680

ISBN-13: 978-1-58270-162-2
ISBN-10:   1-58270-162-8

First Atria Books/Beyond Words hardcover edition March 2007

10 9 8 7 6 5 4 3 2 1

ATRIA B O O K S is a trademark of Simon & Schuster, Inc.

Beyond Words Publishing is a division of Simon & Schuster, Inc.

Manufactured in the United States of America

For more information about special discounts for bulk purchases,
please contact Simon & Schuster Special Sales at
1-800-456-6798 or business@simonandschuster.com.

The corporate mission of Beyond Words Publishing, Inc.: *Inspire to Integrity*

C O N T E N T S

~~~~~~~~

The Positive Energy of Love and Gratitude

What comes to mind when you think of water? Oceans and rivers? Perhaps rain, or the water you drink every day? About 70 percent of this planet that we call home is covered with water, and about 70 percent of the human body is water. Without water, we would not be able to exist, and neither would the earth exist as we know it. Water is as important as it is irreplaceable.

Over the years, I have taken photographs of crystals made by freezing water. But I don't always take pictures of crystals as I find them. I often first expose the water to written words, freeze it, and then compare the various crystals that result.

Different water samples may appear to be all the same, but when one sample is exposed to positive words such as "Thank you" and another sample is exposed to negative words such as "Stupid," the two samples form distinctly different types of crystals. The "Thank you" crystals are balanced and well formed, while the "Stupid" crystals are deformed and broken. The energy of words is reflected in the formation of crystals, and depending on the words, the crystals are either beautiful or unsightly.

Since our bodies consist of 70 percent water, we can infer from the crystals that the water within us also contains the energy of words. It is perhaps not a stretch to think this way, because we often use words such as *thick*, *thin*, *heavy*, and *clean* to describe blood. If you think about water in terms of its quality, then it is easier to understand the energy contained within water.

What can we do to purify all the water within our bodies? I have explained that showing water good words results in the creation of beautiful crystals, and that's the answer. Simply use good words on a daily basis. People whose language is filled with expressions such as "Thank you" and "I love you" have water within them that is pure and beautiful, and likewise, people who use negative expressions such as "You idiot!" and "It's no good" can expect that the water within them will be deformed and distorted.

I am often asked, "What words did you use to create the most beautiful crystal you've ever photographed?" And my answer without hesitation is always, "Love and gratitude." The crystal on the cover of this book happens to be such a crystal. When water is exposed to the words "love and gratitude," it is filled with the most joy. If you look at the crystal on the cover, you'll see why I say this. When you continually think thoughts of love and gratitude, you simply cannot help but be changed. These thoughts will change the water within you, and the result will most certainly be a changed you.

In this book, I will focus on these words—*love and gratitude*—and share some of my ideas for using water's unique role of transporting vibration and resonance to help you welcome change and live a more positive and happy life.

The Balance between Love Given and Gratitude Received

What do you think is the most essential energy necessary for sustaining human life? Love and gratitude, of course. The most important form of energy that we have on this earth is the ability to love someone wholly and purely and to be filled with gratitude when someone rescues us from the edge of despair. You can probably remember a time or two when the energy of love and gratitude has come to you just when you needed it. They are essential forces in our lives.

You might wonder why I didn't show water the words "love" and "gratitude" separately. It was a whim that made me show both words combined, and the resulting crystals were noticeably different. Here's my explanation for why these crystals are the most beautiful: Love is the energy that we give to others, and gratitude is the love that we receive from others. In other words, the greatest form of energy results from the harmony between the energy of giving and the energy of receiving.

To apply this lesson to our own lives, if we hope to use this powerful energy as a guiding force, then just the energy resulting from only giving is not enough, and neither is the energy resulting from only taking. Only when love and gratitude are combined and balanced will they create a beautiful life for us, just as the combination moves the earth and the universe.

Words Are Vibration

When you look at water crystals formed from pure water and crystals formed from impure water, there isn't an easily discernable difference. So if it is not the type of water, what influences crystal formation? The answer is vibration.

Words are a form of vibration. The Bible states, "In the beginning was the Word," and the Japanese have a saying that, roughly translated, means, "Words bring both good and ill fortune." Words and language are an integral part of our collective history.

The words we use evolve over great expanses of time, not unlike the process of evolution evident in nature. Of all the words that have evolved over time, *love and gratitude* are the most beautiful, in my opinion. We all live in pursuit of these virtues. Love and gratitude create the harmony found in all of nature. This harmony is a force so powerful that it is quite likely beyond our ability to understand. Even if we appear to be seeing chaos in the details, the overall effect is one of harmony.

Therefore, while you may not experience an immediate result when you disrupt the balance of love and gratitude, the negative effects will ultimately catch up with you. Pain and sorrow often result. There are times when, due to a lack of love and gratitude, the harmony of the entire human race is thrown into chaos by natural disasters such as earthquakes or tsunamis. My theory is that disastrous phenomena are the result of disruptions in the energy of love and gratitude.

Some might say that this is a preposterous idea. It is true that this theory lacks solid scientific backing, but the starting point for all science can be found in fantasy and dreams. The preposterous idea of yesteryear is the proven science of today. We can never hope to understand the world unless we practice unlimited thinking.

I hope that each person who picks up this book will become aware of the energy of love and gratitude that he or she possesses and then spread that knowledge to others. Those people will be likewise affected and share their experience with even more people. Knowing the power of love and gratitude has the potential to bring happiness to the people around you—and even to all the people of the world.

Join me in exploring the power of words and vibration, and the energy of love and gratitude, in the following pages of this book.

As an example, I often see young women diligently drinking copious amounts of water for their health and beauty. Perhaps they would see better results if they focused on purifying the water that makes up 70 percent of their body by using positive words and thoughts. This, I believe, is the best and quickest way to internal beauty and to physical vitality.

The second lesson that the water-crystal photographs teach us is that no matter how pure and tasty the water you drink, careless words and thoughts have the chance to destroy the beautiful crystals that might have formed. Crystals formed from even the purest water available change daily, depending on the environment and the words that it's exposed to in every moment. Keeping your words positive will keep the water within you pure and beautiful.

The Sounds of Nature

So what are words? I was raised in Japan by parents who spoke Japanese, and that's why I speak Japanese. But if, for example, I was separated from my parents soon after birth and raised by Chinese

3

parents, then my mother tongue would, of course, be Chinese. In other words, no matter how much Japanese blood runs through my veins, it's not going to affect my language or the way I speak. Language is learned and not passed down through our DNA.

If we consider the biblical Adam and Eve, who taught them language? Since they had no earthly parents to teach them, I believe that they learned the first language of humankind by listening to the various vibrations and sounds created by nature.

Nature's sounds are indeed numerous. Just consider all the different sounds made by water in a stream as it flows. At the source, the water *bubbles* out of the ground, and then it *trickles* down and joins other creeks to become a *rushing* stream and perhaps even a *roaring* river that *plunges* over falls. The water may eventually form an expansive river that *hums* slowly toward the sea. With each subtle change in the environment, the sound of water changes as it moves along.

A sudden and radical change in nature, such as an earthquake, volcanic eruption, or tidal wave, is also revealed by sound. The ancient people were more attuned to nature than we are, and they knew what it was telling them. When someone heard the sound of water about to rush over the banks, he or she would need to tell others so they could escape to high ground, and the best way to do it was by imitating the sound of the river. By continuing to listen, they would be able to tell when the rain had stopped and the water had retreated. Likewise, they would have wanted to communicate this to others and to indicate that it was safe to return.

Coincidentally, the word in Sanskrit for "sound" is *Nada-Brahman*. *Nada* means "wide river" and *Brahman* means "the source," indicating the concept that sound is at the source of the river. My name, Emoto, also happens to mean "source of the river" in Japanese, so I guess it would only make sense that I would travel around the world spreading the message of water.

In any case, the sounds of nature come in many forms. Some are pleasurable sounds while others are mournful, and our distant ancestors understood this from what they experienced on a daily basis. They also understood the sounds of calmness, heat, cold, frustration, comfort, large animals, small animals, and males and females. And through imitation, the sounds of nature became our sounds—and our eventual language. See for yourself: Listen to water in a creek, river, lake, or ocean and try to hear the similarities between nature's sounds and our own words.

Differences in Environment Account for Different Words

When you think about the role that nature plays in the formation of language, it makes you wonder if there were ancient words that could not be replaced—words so fundamental to a language that they should not and must not be replaced due to the connection to the unchanging principles of nature.

Yet our world contains many different languages. How did this happen?

The principles that exist in nature exist *everywhere* in nature and always have and always will, but the form of nature changes depending on factors in the environment such as temperature and humidity. This accounts for the differences in languages spoken by different peoples. Japanese, for example, has a large array of descriptive words, which may be a result of a generally homogeneous ethnic group being spread from the frigid northern part of the country to its tropical southern tip. And with distinct seasons throughout most of Japan, the weather is in a constant state of flux. Japan is a country blessed with bountiful nature, filling the air with a rich variety of sounds that would, over time, have become the source of an equally rich variety of words, including those used in distinctive forms of Japanese poetry such as haiku and tanka.

By contrast, the tongue of the Ainu, a distinctive and small minority group living in the most northern part of Japan, includes very few words, although they do have some 160 words to describe water. The part of Japan where most of the Ainu live is known for its many streams and lakes and heavy precipitation. These aspects of nature each have distinctive sounds—sounds that over the years evolved into words.

No matter where you go in the world, nature emits sounds with vibrations distinctive to the particular location and environment, accounting for the many different languages spoken by the various peoples of the earth.

The Formation of Crystals Using Different Languages

Unpleasant and pleasant phenomena witnessed by the ancients were expressed by words that conveyed the nature of the phenomena, i.e., ugly words or beautiful words. And by extension, water exposed to beautiful words forms beautiful crystals, while ugly words form ugly crystals. This should be expected, considering that words came from the sounds or vibrations of nature. The ability to distinguish between the fearful sounds, gentle sounds, enjoyable sounds, and worrisome sounds of nature, and the desire to communicate with others, is where language all began.

But here's something you might not expect. When water is exposed to a word from Japanese, German, English, Korean, or any other language with the same meaning, crystals similar in appearance are formed. "Thank you" and its equivalent expression in Japanese, "Arigato," despite being completely different words, look surprisingly similar as crystals. Why would different words, albeit with similar meanings, have this effect on crystals?

We already know that differences in nature result in the formation of different words. While the sound of the pig in English is *oink-oink*, the sound in Japanese is something like *bu-bu*. While the English-speaking rooster goes *cock-a-doodle-doo*, the Japanese rooster's morning call sounds more like *ko-ke-ko-ko*. The reason for the differences is that the way people who grew up in Japan hear a sound is ever so slightly different from the way people born and raised in a different country perceive that same sound. The pigs and chickens of one country are not that different—perhaps not any different—from the animals found in another country, but the way a culture hears these sounds is different.

Although words of different languages may look and sound different, they are all formed according to the principle of nature. So regardless of the language, when water is exposed to words with similar meanings, the crystals formed are similar.

We Are One with the Universe's Vibrations

The Japanese word for "cosmos," *uchu*, supposedly came from the sounds the stars make. Perhaps the English word "cosmos" was formed based on the same sound. Although there are many different words for the cosmos, there is only one cosmos, and all the different words are perhaps nothing more than different ways of hearing the same thing.

Knowing that words come to us from the vibrations of the universe should help us to see that we are all one. Going about your life with this understanding is completely different from going about your life thinking only of yourself. Being concerned only with the short term is no way to live. Perhaps worrying only about the immediate future is the best some people can do. But when you have worried yourself sick over the immediate future it's important to broaden your perspective and see that the sky is all one and that we are all one with the sky and the cosmos.

Today more and more people seem to feel lost. Young people no longer know what to do with their future. The reason for this feeling of aimlessness and confusion is that the world we have created seems artificial. In this consumer society where everything we see was made by someone else besides us, what's real is what's natural: the sun, the moon, the stars, and plant and animal life. We gain perspective when we consider these natural wonders. All of us who feel lost can find direction by remembering that we all feel the universe's vibrations and by taking comfort in the common roots of our language.

Changing Yourself with Your Words

Think about the words you use day in and day out. Your words and the way you use them have an important influence on what kind of life you live. This isn't a discovery that's going to catch anyone by surprise.

Words are vibrations, and when our bodies, with all the water coursing through them, are exposed to good words, we cannot help but experience health and well-being. And in the same way, bad words and their bad vibrations will predictably have a negative effect on our bodies, so we should not be surprised when destructive words destroy.

So much can ride on a single word. That's why your life's outcome depends on how you use words and how you relate to their meaning each and every day. More so today than in the past, we are surrounded by negative words on the radio, on television, and in conversation with others. While some negative language used for humor may not be so bad, much of the language we use, and even many of the new words and expressions that enter our language through modern culture, are negative in their vibration.

It is within our power to shift our shared lexicon to the positive. You can start with yourself.

Improving Your State of Mind
with Crystals

Let's take a closer look at some crystals. Look through the crystal photographs in this book and ask yourself which is the most beautiful. The crystal that you think is the most beautiful is the symbol of what you most desire. That is what your heart is searching for and what it wants to resonate with. If, for example, you think the "exhilaration" crystal is the most beautiful, then exhilaration is what you need in your life. You can choose to wake up in the morning and go about your life with exhilaration, even feeling exhilarated by what you eat. If you live your life that way for seven to ten days, you can be sure that your life will become more exhilarating. At that time you can open this book and again ask yourself which crystal you find the most beautiful. Maybe then you'll choose the "hope" crystal, in which case you would go about your daily life with hope being your predominant thought and feeling.

Place your selected crystal's picture in a spot where you can look at it several times a day. Frame or stand the photograph where you can see it out of the corner of your eye as you go about your day. Every time you gaze at it, you will align with the vibrations of love and gratitude, and you will achieve the feeling you desire. You might want to put the "You're beautiful!" crystal next to your mirror as a reminder to appreciate yourself. Or perhaps place the "love and gratitude" crystal near the bathtub where you wash away your fatigue and worries. Surrounding yourself with water-crystal photographs brings a ray of sunshine into your life.

You can change your life by looking at the crystal photographs. No two photographs of crystals are exactly the same. And maybe this is one reason why these photographs have the power to relax and heal. They are one of a kind, and so offer a unique vibration. Even simply having them nearby will create vibrations with which you can resonate.

Let the precious water within your heart become like beautiful crystals. That is where all change begins.

Words of Energy for Achieving Dreams

What is the true message of individual words? What message is hidden in words that can change your life? You can find clues to the answer to these questions and others in water crystals.

The crystal on page 36 was taken after the water was exposed to "I can do it." Solid and beautiful, the crystal seems to be telling us that if we believe we can do something, we can find a way to make it happen, even if it seems impossible. So if your boss says to you, "It's a really tough job, but I'd like you to do it," the outcome will depend on whether you say "I can do it" to your boss and yourself.

Saying words out loud creates the energy you need to accomplish the task in a focused and efficient way. Even if you're all alone when you say it, the water within your body will respond to this powerful affirmation and provide just the right support to get the task done.

In Japanese, words have a spirit. Thinking about words as having a spirit may help us understand their power. One thing I have noticed through research and life experience is that you can better use the spirit of words to help you achieve your dreams by using the past tense. In other words, it's even better to say "I did it" than "I can do it." Saying the same thing as if it has already happened seems to bring about an especially strong level of energy to any effort.

The next time you embark on a goal, try saying, "I did such and such" rather than "I can do such and such." Speaking in the past tense when faced with a difficult task can make all the difference.

By contrast, if you think you can't do something, you'll probably be right, no matter how easy the task may actually be. This seems to be the message of the "I can't do it" crystal found on page 37. "I can do it" results in a beautiful crystal, while "I can't do it" results in a distorted crystal. However, if you make an effort, you can see in the distorted crystal the possibility of a beautiful crystal forming.

If you maintain a strong desire, then the people around you will come to your aid. The worst thing you can do is say, "I can't do it."

Why is it that negative statements such as "I can't do it" and "I won't do it" result in deformed crystals? I'm convinced from my research that it is because these concepts are not found anywhere in nature. The power that created our planet and our universe incorporated perfect and complete harmony and purposefulness. Everything that exists is in a constant state of recirculation. A leaf, for example, falls to the ground and returns to the soil to provide nourishment to the tree from whence it came. Such an environment, where everything has a purpose, leaves no room for vibrations of "I can't do it."

Words of Encouragement to Others for Yourself

When you're thinking about attempting a goal for the first time and you lack confidence, the words "You can do it" have special significance. But when you're venturing into unknown territory, other people are unlikely to give you this encouragement. Instead you might hear, "You're not serious?"

or "You don't really think you can do it, do you?" At a time when you need all the confidence you can muster, such words have a negative effect on both the person who hears them and the person who says them.

This is closely related to the main theme of this book: the power and resonance of words. For example, *love and gratitude*: We do know that love comes from the inside and spreads out, and that gratitude is the feeling felt by the receiver of this vibration. However, as I mentioned previously, the person who receives love and feels confidence will then be in a position to emit love, and in this way, love and gratitude spread throughout the world with the vibration of this beautiful energy.

So when you say to someone, "You can do it," you have done a great service not only to that person but also to yourself. When the response is something like, "When you say that, it makes me feel like I really can do it, and I will," then the energy will come back to you and the can-do vibration will fill you with confidence.

Now, if you had instead said, "Are you sure?" then what would happen? The other person's confidence would be crushed, filling the space with negative vibrations, and you, likewise, would be filled with uncertainty. This is why, whenever you can, it makes more sense to speak positive words than negative words. Another case in point can be found by looking at the crystal on page 39: "Everything is going to work out."

It seems to form two crystals. Perhaps we can see the overlaying of the feelings of the person who says the words and the person who hears them. You can imagine someone saying, "I know you're worried, but I'm behind you so give it a try."

Any words that give positive energy to another are certain to result in positive energy for the giver. Try this out at home, with your co-workers, and with your friends—you'll surely see results. If your words shine a light on those around you, you won't have to walk in the dark.

The Rewards of Making Others Happy

The crystals formed by "happiness" and "dislike" on pages 40 and 41 form an interesting contrast. The "happiness" crystal looks somewhat like a happy crab with hornlike formations on its hexagonal body. The "dislike" crystal looks similar to the "happy" crystal, but it appears as if it was squashed in its growth process.

To explore the differences, let's consider for a moment what makes people feel the happiest. Of course, we are happy when we are paid a compliment or given a gift. But I suspect that most people are happiest when they do something for someone that causes happiness for that person. There's nothing that makes me happier than to see a happy face and to know that this person looks that way because of me.

This, again, is a phenomenon of the love and gratitude that I've mentioned. What's happening is that the feeling of gratitude which the receiver has toward the giver changes form and becomes love. When you understand the happiness that comes from giving, the circle of happiness around you will spread.

The Japanese word for "happiness" is *ureshii*, which is written with a Japanese character formed by two parts. The first means "woman" and the second means "good fortune." Perhaps the ancients who created the writing system used in Japan knew something about how important it is to make other people, and maybe women in particular, happy. And in fact, the crab-looking crystal seems to resemble a smiling woman.

However, the "dislike" crystal looks like the face of someone who has taken a bite of something bitter. As long as you look at people in such a way, you will continue to dislike them. But if you make a special effort to smile at the people you dislike, you'll soon sense that your feelings of dislike are dissipating.

Certainly there are some people whom I don't much care for, but I know that I shouldn't carry feelings of dislike within me. It only hurts me in the end. So what can we do to get rid of negative feelings? Here's my suggestion. If you harbor feelings of dislike toward someone, that person will likely also have negative feelings toward you. If you can think that the cause for the dislike lies within you and ponder how that person might be feeling toward you, then you're halfway to solving the problem.

The next step is to think about how you might be responsible for the different vibrations within that person and then to approach that person again with your negative feelings in check. You might be surprised to discover that all your dislike for that person has suddenly disappeared. Also, if you find yourself in a situation where you're alone with someone you dislike, bring a third party into the meeting. I've found that while two people might result in a conflicting frequency, a third person often brings everyone's energy into harmony.

Instead of giving up on improving relations with someone you dislike, try the methods I've mentioned and you might just surprise yourself with a change of heart.

Be Generous with Compliments

Any type of compliment helps create a beautiful crystal. The crystal created by "You tried hard" on page 44 is beautiful and perhaps a little restrained. Let's say that a child needs to study for an hour, but after thirty minutes you can see that he or she can study no more. You say, "You tried hard." What would the child think as a result of this encouraging statement? *I thought I would get in trouble for studying only thirty minutes, but I actually got complimented. If I study more, I might get complimented even more.*

So even a half-compliment can do much more to encourage someone than other expressions such as "Try harder" and "Keep at it." Expressions such as these usually result more in pressure than encouragement. While verbal pressure might result in more study time, it's not likely to result in more motivation. Crystals created by complimentary words seem to support this deduction.

This doesn't just go for children. Instead of telling co-workers and family members to work harder, you can compliment them for trying hard. You will be doing them the favor of energizing the water within them.

This strategy is especially important when you are in a leadership position. When you want improvement, you could demand it directly. However, often a more effective approach is to compliment first and then suggest what could be improved. For example, "You did a nice job. I like what you've done. But maybe you could..." While we often say that a leader leads by example, it's important not to underestimate the power of words.

For an example of what happens when you criticize, look at the crystal on page 44 made by "It's hopeless." Perhaps you know someone who has a habit of saying, "It's hopeless," or "It's not going to work out." Their words create their future, and every possibility they encounter will have a negative outcome.

There are some people who can take bad news and use it to give them the energy they need to try even harder. For most of us, the best we can do is to avoid bad news. Negative information relays negative vibration, often resulting in a negative chain reaction that at times can lead to a fight, a crime, or perhaps even a war—all things that should be avoided when possible.

But ask yourself this: Why do so many people get enjoyment from watching mean-spirited television shows and hearing malicious gossip about celebrities? What they really get out of this is bad vibration rather than any true enjoyment. When you expose yourself unnecessarily to unhappy vibration, you put your own happiness at risk.

Wouldn't it be much wiser to wish happiness for others as much as you wish happiness for yourself? If everyone did this, the world would indeed be a wonderful place.

Finding Your Natural State of Wellness and Enjoyment

Water crystals also teach us about returning to our natural state: enjoying life and experiencing wellness.

Take a look at the "energetic" crystal on page 42. This healthy and well-balanced crystal seems to be telling us the importance of being healthy and energetic. When we make that choice, we fill the water within our bodies with energy. The "exhaustion" crystal on page 43, on the other hand, looks tired and worn out. When you say you're tired, the water within your body responds accordingly.

The Japanese word for "energetic," perhaps also translated as "health," is written with two characters: 元気. The first means the "source" or "origin," and the second refers to "energy" or "spirit." Our original state is health, and it's only natural that we return to this state and be healthy. If we are not healthy, then we have, somewhere along the way, gotten out of rhythm. For human beings, this energy or natural state of health is the starting point, and it's the point to which we need to continually return. Keep a photograph of the "energetic" crystal close by to help bring you back to your natural state of wellness.

When I exposed water to the word "enjoyment" to make the crystal on page 45, I anticipated a lively and vibrant crystal, but the crystal is actually quite conservative and basic. Perhaps this crystal is telling us that enjoyment is something that's quite normal, something that should catch no one by surprise. "Enjoyment," as well as "energetic," produced a surprisingly typical crystal, and why should we think these elements aren't a typical part of our daily life?

The act of living itself is an act of enjoyment. Some might argue, "That's not true. Life is full of pain." But think about this: At the moment of conception within your mother's womb, one of between 100 million and 400 million sperm was the one to fertilize your mother's egg. That already makes you an exceptional being to begin with. Now you, as the chosen one, carry the responsibility to live and enjoy life to the fullest.

The most natural life we can live is the one that is most enjoyable—and also the one that is best for our bodies. Here's an interesting way I look at it from my Japanese point of view.

The word for "enjoyment" in Japanese is written with the character 楽. If you add an element or "radical" that means "grass" to the top of this character, then the resulting character becomes "medicine": 薬. And medicine is what is used to restore the body and mind to a state where enjoyment is once again possible. The "grass" radical at the top refers to nature, and so we might also deduce that when you live close to nature, your body will be healthier and better able to enjoy life. Nature, water, and our natural state of wellness and enjoyment are forever linked.

Keep On Dreaming

When you look at the "Dreams come true" crystal on page 45, you'll see that it looks somewhat like the "enjoyment" crystal, although it is considerably more complex. This seems to indicate that our dreams are of a different dimension, accounting for the multiple layers seen in the crystal.

Human beings have evolved over the ages in order to achieve their dreams, and this is our natural evolution. Having a dream pushes you forward. Take a moment and think about your dream. It might be a big dream or a little dream. Maybe it's a dream that others would laugh at. Don't worry about what others think. Strive for your dream, and when you accomplish it or even a small part of it, celebrate! You will now be able to move ahead with more confidence than before, and soon you'll find your next dream, and on it goes.

When I was a small boy, I told my friends that my dream was to become the Secretary General of the United Nations. That's not the direction I pursued in life, but that dream still occupies a corner of my mind. Perhaps it's the water within my body that remembers it, and perhaps that's why I have created two opportunities in the last few years to give speeches at the United Nations.

Your body remembers your dreams, which is why it is important to speak your dream. It will help you find the way to make the impossible possible. If all the people around the globe speak their dream of world peace, ten years from now that heretofore unachievable dream will be closer to being a reality.

~~~~~~~~~~~~~~~

CHAPTER THREE

Understanding Vibration and Resonance

I n this chapter, we will take a further look at the way our words vibrate and resonate between ourselves and others. Let me first explain more about vibration, the force that moves us.

The Vibration of Existence

When we think about the factors necessary for survival, at the top of the list will come breathing, and in order to breathe, we need oxygen. We also need water, food, and sleep. Without an almost constant supply of these elements, survival would be impossible. What do these elements all have in common? The answer is energy.

We are talking about this same energy when we say things like, "I don't seem to have any energy." If we really didn't have any energy, we wouldn't be able to survive, and neither would anything else that exists on this planet. Whether we're sitting, standing, working, or playing, everything we do requires energy. In order to regain the energy lost through activity, we need sleep. And so the sustenance of life requires a constant and consistent combination of oxygen, water, food, and sleep.

We can't talk about energy without talking about vibration. Without vibration, we would be unable to create energy. Vibration is what makes it possible for everything to exist. All that exists is in a state of vibration, and this is the source of energy.

Vibration, the Energy of Life

Imagine an object vibrating. Perhaps you can almost hear the sound of it moving back and forth. Scientists tell us that everything vibrates, and thus everything emits sound—even the pebble lying alongside the road, even though you might pick it up and hear nothing.

The human ear is capable of hearing sounds within the range of approximately 15 to 20,000 hertz. One hertz is equivalent to one vibration per second. Human beings cannot hear anything with a vibration higher or lower than that range. So just because you can't hear a sound doesn't mean a sound isn't being made. As long as a little pebble exists alongside the road, it is vibrating, and that vibration is making sound, no matter how small.

This concept was perhaps better understood by the ancients than by the people of today. A Buddhist saying speaks of Kannon, the goddess of mercy and compassion, as being capable of seeing all and feeling all. All existence is vibration and sound, and vibration is life itself. Without vibration, we would not exist.

The Japanese write the word "life" using the character 命. At the top of the character, you can see a roof, and under the roof is a person sleeping, symbolized by a horizontal line. Under the sleeping person are two symbols that, when combined, refer to "tapping." We might compare this to the creation of vibration and, thus, the formation of life.

This life force that makes our existence possible is the same life force that makes possible the existence of the pebble alongside the road. To say that something exists is to say it vibrates, and everything that vibrates has life.

Vibration by Way of Water

We now understand that without vibration, it would be impossible for us to live, but since when was simple survival enough? Human beings differentiate themselves from other life forms by seeking a quality of life and happiness in addition to survival. And that leads us on the search for what makes us happy.

I have found in my studies that the phenomenon of resonance causes happiness. Resonance is simply the act of vibration resulting in more vibration. It requires the interaction of two complementary objects or energies. These energies are referred to in the Chinese culture as *yin* and *yang*, or light and dark—or, as I believe, love and gratitude. The love given and the gratitude returned resonate with each other through the vibration of giving and the gratitude of receiving.

Perhaps when you were a child you conducted an experiment using two tuning forks. When one tuning fork is struck to make a vibrating sound, the other tuning fork placed nearby starts to make the same sound. This is resonance, and in order for it to work, the two objects need to have the same number of vibrations; they need to be on the same frequency. If the two tuning forks are of different frequencies, no matter how hard you strike one, it won't have any effect on the other.

It's not hard to see why something vibrates when you strike it, but it takes some thinking to understand why one object vibrates when you strike a completely separate object. It's a simple experiment, but it is eloquent in expressing the fundamental characteristics of energy.

Let me explain this more thoroughly. If vibration is energy, then resonance is the reverberation of energy, and resonance is thus capable of relaying energy. When you shout in a tunnel, you can hear your voice echoing. This is also a form of resonance. In order for resonance to be created in the tunnel, you need to shout first. In other words, energy cannot be relayed unilaterally. It requires the resonance of two elements, elements such as two friends, parent and child, or husband and wife.

The energy that is all around us wasn't always there. It is the resonance from earlier times passed down to us today. When we trace the energy back to the beginning of this resonance, we will reach the point at the very moment when this universe was created, that very first vibration. Who made this vibration? It was the creator of this universe, however you refer to this being or force. At the moment of the universe's conception, the creator made the first vibration. When this vibration met with vibrations of the same frequency, resonance resulted and energy was created. The vibration continued to resonate and create energy. Thus, the creator used the medium of resonance to create this universe.

Something was required to transmit the energy of resonance necessary for creation, and that substance was water. Water was instrumental for forming and sustaining life, just as it is today. Think of water as a train that transports vibration. Without

"Exhilaration"

"Dream"

"Peace"

"Love and gratitude"

These photographs were taken from water frozen after being placed in four different glass containers with the words taped to the sides. It's easy to see how such positive words would yield these beautiful crystals.

"I can do it."

Approach new adventures with a feeling of self-confidence. What you need to do to succeed will become clear. If you have a vision, then there's little else to worry about.

"I can't do it."

You can't if you think you can't. If you keep on trying and don't give up, you might discover that people around you will come to your aid when you need it the most.

"It's going to be all right."

This crystal seems to be beaming with reassurance, like a child full of innocent buoyancy.

"Everything is going to work out."

It looks like someone has told this crystal that it's good to try and that a helping hand is always nearby.

"Happiness"

With six legs and two eyes, doesn't this crystal resemble a crab with a joyful face?

"Dislike"

The difference between this crystal and the "happiness" crystal is striking. It looks like this crystal has bitten into something bitter. When you harbor thoughts of dislike, then dislike is internalized. A smile is the best thing to give to those you dislike.

"Energetic"

Your health comes from within, and it is affected by your words.
If you want to make the water within your body as vibrant as this
crystal, then it is important to tell yourself, "I feel great!"

"Exhaustion"

Even saying "exhaustion" makes the water within your body look worn and withered. If you find yourself saying this out of habit, try shifting your thinking.

"You tried hard."

Words of encouragement always seem to form beautiful crystals.
This crystal is well formed, but it appears a little restricted.

"It's hopeless."

Negative words have an immediate, disastrous effect on crystals.
Think twice before exposing yourself to negative thoughts.

"Enjoyment"

You might expect the "enjoyment" crystal to be more playful and energetic, but this appears to be a rather solid geometric crystal. For water, enjoyment is a completely natural state. You might say that truth can be found in enjoyment.

"Dreams come true."

Dreams form a world of their own, and so it seems that this crystal has created a multi-layered shape with rings and light orbiting around it, possibly indicating a dream come to life.

"You're beautiful!" said repeatedly to water yielded this crystal.

"Isolate, ignore"

"Your beautiful!" said sometimes to water yielded this crystal.

Crystals receive even more damage from being ignored than from being exposed to degrading words.

"Beautiful"

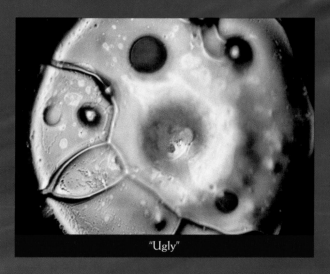

"Ugly"

Even thinking of yourself or someone else as ugly rather than beautiful can cause considerable damage.

"Hope"

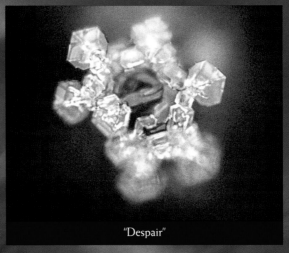

"Despair"

The "hope" crystal appears to have first been tiny, and then it grew into a big and beautiful crystal. Hope can grow and expand with age and experience. The "despair" crystal seems to have created two hexagonal crystals, possibly indicating that new hope can be found within despair.

"Adoration"

"Eternal"

"Clasping hands"

Do you know someone who can have a healing effect on you just by being nearby? "Adoration" results in an untainted crystal full of life. The "eternal" crystal creates a well-formed hexagonal crystal, almost as a symbol of eternal resonance. "Clasping hands" creates a crystal that appears willing to share its energy.

"Dad"

"Mom"

"Mom" takes a softer bundle of a shape than "dad."

"Convenience foods"

"Home cooking"

Compared to "home cooking," "convenience foods" does not even cause the water crystals to form a hexagonal shape.

sufficient water, the energy of vibration will not be able to flow throughout the body. Since vibration is the source of energy, energy would have no way to enter the body without water, and death would be not far behind.

This may not be the way everyone sees it, but more than ten years of research and water-crystal photography has convinced me that water's role is to transport vibration—energy—to the body. More and more people recently seem to be coming to this way of thinking.

Water is not only critical for sustaining life, but it is also necessary for keeping a good outlook on life. I have observed that people who are dehydrated soon lose their sense of humor. It so happens that the words "humor" and "humidity" come from the same Latin word. Even the ancients understood that with sufficient water, people are lighthearted and can enjoy humor, but humor wanes when humidity dwindles. In fact, when humidity drops by 50 percent, life is no longer sustainable. The vibration carried by water is nothing more or less than energy. If we only have half as much water as we need, we'll only have half as much energy as we need, and at that level, we'll not only be unable to resonate, we'll also be unable to vibrate.

By understanding that life is vibration, you'll also see that life after death is possible. Because vibration is life, life does not require a body in order to continue. Think of the body as little more than a tuxedo or dress that you rent for a short period of time. You'll need to return your tuxedo or dress when the time is up, but that fact alone does not mean the end of vibration. The soul, freed of the body, continues to vibrate, making life eternal.

In the next chapter, I'll explain how the principle of resonance can be applied to your daily life to improve your communication, relationships, and health.

CHAPTER FOUR

Using Resonance in
Your Daily Life

Perhaps the greatest role that water plays in sustaining life is the transportation of vibration, and the greatest role of vibration is resonance. Resonance is not possible in a vacuum; for people to resonate, they require someone with the same vibration.

Resonance can occur among unrelated people without them even knowing. The British biologist Rupert Sheldrake gives us an example of how written or spoken words can have an effect on other unrelated people all over the world. According to his theory of "morphic resonance," when a person begins something new, if it's good and wholesome then the words of that person will go to other people who have similar consciousnesses.

To study this theory, he divided fans of the hugely popular and difficult *London Times* crossword puzzle into two types: those who worked on the puzzle as soon as they got it on Saturday evening, and those who waited until later to do it. The people who waited until later to work on the puzzle did significantly better than those who worked on it right away.

Perhaps what was happening was that when someone filled in a word, the vibration of the word blended into the fabric of the universe and then was attracted to people who resonated with the same appreciation for crossword puzzles. The phenomenon of resonance affects us all, wherever we are.

While we often resonate with people we aren't even aware of, we resonate on a daily basis with people directly connected to our lives—friends and loved ones. Through this resonance, love and gratitude are exchanged, and energy is created. Because

resonance is similar to communication, fully understanding it will help you improve your relationships
and communication in all aspects of life.

Resonance for Better Communication

Perfect resonance would make the ideal relationship possible, but people will inevitably have different frequencies. If two people vibrate on vastly
different frequencies, it will soon become evident
that they need distance between them, and that
will take care of the problem. However, when two
people's frequency is only slightly different, then it
can cause all sorts of problems.

You see this phenomenon at play in many relationship problems among in-laws. The frequencies
of a husband and a mother-in-law, for example, are
probably not so different, since they both, at the very
least, share a love for the same person. But sometimes even small differences in frequency can create
disharmony. The same thing can occur in relationships between co-workers and acquaintances.

To help you get over hurdles in these kinds of
relationships, think about a piano keyboard. It consists of black and white keys, each one essential to

the formation of the keyboard, just as everything in our world is essential. When played together, some of the keys result in harmony, while other keys of different values result in a sound that is quite unpleasant. For example, the sounds of *do* and *mi*, *do* and *fa*, and *do* and *so* are able to create resonance. But *do* and *re*, sounds that are close to each other, result in a disharmonious sound.

Like the harmonious chords of *do-mi-so*, when people talk with others with whom they naturally resonate, the result is harmony. But what should you do when you have to be with someone with whom you don't resonate, say a co-worker or mother-in-law? Try adding another person to the mix. When two people just don't seem to be able to communicate, another person can help harmonize the energies.

Another way to improve relationships is to align your frequency with the frequency of the person you don't get along with. How? Stand in the shoes of that person and try to see the world through his or her eyes. In order to do that, you need to know that person rather well. If you know someone's interests, family situation, and past, then you can put yourself in that person's place and see why he or she is thinking and behaving that way. With the passing of time, people grow and change, and someone you initially rejected might eventually seem not so bad. Consciously and continuously put yourself in the same frequency as another in order to resonate with them. When you become capable of that, then you will be able to share love and gratitude with that person, and the relationship can be mutually fulfilling and nourishing.

By becoming fully aware that your vibration is a living thing, you can become far more skilled at getting along in the world.

Friendship and Resonance

As you can see on page 90, water crystals that were formed by being shown the word "friend" were extremely beautiful and reflected happiness. Moreover, when we look at the concept of "a circle of friends," we observe that when you make one friend, then, one by one, you make more friends.

Your friends are like a mirror in which you can see a reflection of yourself. By extension, if you notice particular good points in your friends, it's quite possible that you are lacking these "good points" in yourself. Your friends exist for the important purpose of assisting your growth.

If you are able to express yourself freely on a variety of issues with friends, then it can be said that you are "open." If you are not open to having discussions with friends about a wide variety of matters, then you are closing yourself off from receiving new knowledge and wisdom. How about making a fresh start today? Henceforth, start to think of your friends as a mirror in which you are able to see your own reflection, and be open to freely exchanging ideas, emotions, and knowledge.

I count myself lucky to have friends who are older than me, friends who are about the same age, and friends who are younger than me. In my organization, there are members of the staff with whom I associate and whom I consider to be my friends. Generally, I am the kind of person who is quick to make new friends regardless of age. I receive energy from these new friends because of the phenomenon of resonance, and this energy helps me continue living in a healthy manner.

Having a huge number of friends is not so important; the main thing is to have high-quality friendships with any number of people you feel comfortable with. This is what makes people happy. I feel that the most important condition of friendship is to be able to hold heart-to-heart discussions with your friends. The ability of people to talk and share ideas with each other is of critical importance, and I feel that people who are unable to do so become part of the cause of various social problems. Finally, in order to bring meaning to your discussions with friends, you need to possess compassion and kindness. Then you will experience the full benefits of energy resonance.

It's Important to Resonate with Other People, Not with Electromagnetic Fields

It seems that something has been changing in the world in recent times: there are people who seem impossible to resonate with, despite one's best efforts—such as the type of person who chooses to sit in front of the television and become reclusive, and as a result becomes adverse to communicating with or relating to others.

A major reason for this type of behavior can be found in the electromagnetic fields around us. There can be no doubt that the diverse electromagnetic fields have a negative impact on human beings. Cell phones, televisions, computers, and other electronic devices surround us all the time. When people have weakened immune systems, the electromagnetic fields they surround themselves with may be strong enough to alter their consciousness.

Let's look at the relationship between the human nervous system and computers. The building blocks for computer systems are 0s and 1s, and these two digits are used to provide all the instructions required by the computer to operate. In other words, it is like a world of *yes–no* choices. When we are constantly exposed to the electromagnetic fields of computers, our bodies and our nervous systems begin to harmonize with the machines. Take a look at the photographs on page 98 to see the effects of these devices on water.

The human nervous system is formed by a vastly diverse number of building blocks, making it possible for us to express a vast range of emotions, including even the level of love and gratitude.

However, when our bodies begin to harmonize with the electromagnetic field emitted by computers, all sorts of things can happen. Most notably, we lose our ability to harmonize with other people around us. Perhaps you know someone who spends an unhealthy amount of time in chat rooms and mail messaging and have witnessed this phenomenon firsthand.

I venture to say that electromagnetic fields are like synthetic spirit. I believe that the spirit of these machines has the potential to attach to our own spirit and drain us of our energy and health. If you find yourself feeling less energetic than you used to be or than you would like to be, first consider the electromagnetic fields created by the electronic devices around you. Whenever the vibration within your body becomes weak, there will be an equivalent weakening of your health and your energy. If you want to increase your energy, look at what's giving you energy—in other words, what you are resonating with. For the well-being of ourselves and the planet, it is critical that we seek to harmonize with other people rather than with the electronic devices that are so ubiquitous in our lives.

Achieving True Love

It is one thing to lack resonance with a co-worker or acquaintance, but falling out of resonance with your own life is another matter entirely. Two people fall in love and form a relationship so close they think it will last forever, but then one or both partners change and sweetness turns to bitterness. In time the relationship ends. It can happen to the best of couples.

When one person changes and the other is unable to detect the change, disharmony is sure to follow. The way to prevent this from happening is simply to continually strive to understand the other person's feelings. Keeping your frequencies aligned depends on striving to see things from your partner's point of view—to change together. If you still find you are unable to resonate with your partner, try putting some space between yourselves. With the distance you need, you may discover who you really are and find how you want to live your life. And then eventually you might be able to return to the situation as before and live in harmony by maintaining your identity and the right amount of space.

To sustain any close relationship, to achieve true love, you need to understand the relationship between love and gratitude and to be willing to show more love and more gratitude.

Loving continually is the secret of happiness—in a relationship, in your career, in yourself. The reason I can say this is because my greatest happiness comes when I give love to someone and they respond with simple gratitude. Love is a feeling of caring and compassion toward the entirety of our world—everyone and everything. Love is sending out vibrations of caring and compassion. Love is the ability to sympathize and empathize with others in a way that makes them a little bit happier.

For some, love and gratitude doesn't get expressed easily. If this sounds like you, even starting out by faking it is all right. Simply saying the words "love and gratitude" more often or writing them in a place where you can see them is a positive step. You might try writing "love and gratitude" on your coffee mug; each time you look at it, you will feel that energy. Do anything you can do to expose yourself to the vibration of love and gratitude.

Once you give love and gratitude a chance to take hold in your own heart, you will be able to experience the joyousness of resonating love and gratitude with others.

CHAPTER FIVE

Water Crystals Can Bring Forth Your Potential

Photographs for Positive Change

We have already seen how resonance results in harmonious vibration and an increase in positive energy. I frequently have the opportunity to meet with people who say to me, "I want to change." As you already understand from the various photographs of water crystals, positive words result in positive change, and we can also conclude that if we wish to make a positive change within ourselves, we will need to change the purity of the water within our bodies.

Perhaps you've seen card decks printed with positive messages. The idea is to pick a card from the deck each morning and then live your life in accordance with the card's message that day. In this same way, I encourage you to look at one of the positive photographs in this book each morning or to use the *Water Crystal Oracle* that I have created (see www.beyondword.com).

In this chapter, we'll look at each crystal and explore the meaning of words and how the meaning is reflected in the crystals. We'll see how each crystal has its own distinct character and unique beauty.

The Amazing Power of Unconscious Words

What do you say to *yourself* each day when you look into the mirror? What words are stirring within your soul? How many of us say such things as "I'm so beautiful" or "I'm really charming"?

Take a look at the crystal at the top of page 47 and you'll see the effect that words such as "beautiful" and "charming" can have. Perhaps you're used to using these words when referring to others, but these are also words that you can say to *yourself.* Keep on talking like that and soon the water within you will change and you will become a truly beautiful person from the inside out.

Now consider the crystal at the bottom of page 47. This crystal appears isolated and ignored. In another experiment conducted with rice, we discovered that rice which was ignored spoiled more rapidly than rice which was exposed to words of scorn. From this, we can deduce that apathy about your body, face, or personality cannot help but have a negative effect. Apathy will spoil the water within us, and from the inside out, the cells will age and deteriorate at an accelerated rate. But if you wish to slow down this process, then become aware of your absolute beauty and appreciate and love every body part, from the top of your head to the tips of your toes.

Just as words have the power to generate energy, so does the casual gaze. When someone looks at you in a positive way, it can do wonders for the way you feel, while being ignored seems to suck the energy from you. In the same way, when you look at yourself in a positive way, you will feel positive energy fill your body, while ignoring yourself will have the opposite effect. If you can see the beauty within yourself, that's the direction in which you'll move. But if all you can see is what you think makes you unattractive, then that is what you'll become more like.

The Power of Desire

As a child, I once made a hundred wishes. Upon those fulfilled dreams of a child, I have built the dreams that I now have as an adult. It is important to have big dreams and to desire with passion. By having big dreams, you will meet the people you need to meet, have the experiences you need to have, and your capacity will rise to the level of your dreams. The bigger your dream, the bigger your capacity will be.

I'm quite sure that everyone who has met with some degree of success in his or her life could tell you something similar to this. Expressions such as "I want this to happen" or "I want to do that" are born of the abilities that you already have. There isn't anything you can honestly wish for that isn't somehow possible.

Have the biggest dreams possible. Big dreamers live bold and full lives. They may get discouraged at times, but they soon succeed. Perhaps this is what the "hope" crystal on page 48 is telling us. One unique thing about this crystal is that it formed and grew at an incredibly fast speed, telling us that hope, even a little hope, will lead to more hope and more possibilities.

Wouldn't it be wonderful to live in such a way that your hopes and dreams continually expand and branch out? I encourage you to place the photograph of this crystal in a place where you can see it as you go about achieving the dreams within your heart.

The Meaning of Dreams

Water that was shown the word "dream" formed a crystal with a beautiful seven-sided shape (see page 35). To me, this seven-point crystal symbolizes a bridge to the fourth dimension, or the future. I believe that dreams possess an unusual dimensional aspect—namely, that they are between the third and fourth dimensions. In other words, they suggest the future but are not a full representation of the fourth dimension. For this reason, I say that they are part of a 3.5 dimensional world, and the seven-point water crystals formed by "dreams" are also part of this world. The world inhabited by the souls of the departed is also made up of 3.5 dimensions.

We always dream, but the dreams themselves are illusory and often fade into nothingness soon after we awaken. These imprecise, seven-sided water crystals formed by being exposed to "dreams" are part of an in-between world. If we look at phenomena from the world of 3.5 dimensions, these phenomena might also serve as a kind of blueprint for a new future.

Let me explain: In Japan it is believed that dreams transcend limitations of time and space. Through our dreams, we are able to receive communications from previous ages and from our own previous lives. Dreams, then, are a form of reference material that provide us with an almost godlike capacity to understand the future.

Lately in my dreams I see the world coming to an end. Because our dreams give us access to memories from previous generations, we have been given the appointed mission of not allowing the same bad things from the past to be repeated. These dreams give me the resolve to change the direction that civilization is headed.

On this point, through water, an appeal is being made for world peace. Through your dreams, you are able to guide yourself. If you have good dreams, those are the kinds of things that will come to pass. When you experience a bad dream, it should be your hope that the contents of that dream will not come to pass. If the terrible things that you dreamt about are actually coming true, then it is up to you to avoid those undesirable things as you go about your daily life. Because it is good that happy occurrences take place, you should set your life's compass to move in a positive direction.

What I am suggesting here is that dreams give us the opportunity and power to control what we do. We can use this power for positive change in the world. This is the belief system that currently guides my life.

Vocalizing Your Dreams for Stronger Effect

How often do you express positive words rather than just letting them float in and out of your consciousness? The water crystals show us the effect that the simple act of vocalizing good words can have.

When we compare water that has been exposed to words only and water exposed to music, the water exposed to music forms into a crystal much faster. Water exposed for only about thirty minutes to music will form crystals that reflect the music, but the formation of the crystal affected by a written word requires at least one day of exposure. It makes sense: music creates and relays considerably more vibration than that created by writing.

To understand the strength of vibration, think about the volume of a speaker. Music is like a speaker turned to high volume, relaying vibration in a direct way. When I previously suggested that you look at yourself in the mirror and compliment yourself, I suggested that you speak out loud instead of just thinking the thoughts, and that also is a direct way of relaying vibration. Perhaps you think that saying "I love you" or "I respect you" to yourself in the mirror just isn't something you could actually do, but I can promise you that people who are capable of changing themselves for the better are all capable of this simple task. When you become accustomed to this, you'll be able to make changes within yourself that, while not initially noticeable, will nonetheless be real through the water within your body.

Let's take another look at the "ugly" crystal on page 47, which effectively reveals what the word "ugly" can do to us. Considering that just thinking "ugly" has this effect, can you imagine the effect it can have on you when you vocalize it? Avoid casting judgment on yourself, other people, or other things by calling them "ugly."

Despair Is the Beginning of Hope

Life is full of mistakes and failure. We sometimes think that everything that can go wrong usually does—the person you love rejects you, the place where you wanted to work doesn't hire you. If you thought about ending your life every time you failed, life would be short indeed.

But let's look at the crystal formed by the word "despair" on page 48. The formation could hardly be called a crystal. This experiment resulted in one or two scrawny crystals, but that was all. What could this be telling us? I think the message is that despair is the beginning of hope. Of course, you experience great sadness at times of despair, but it's also an opportunity to go back to and start again with a clean slate. It's the starting point of *new* hope.

Crystals teach us that by looking at despair in this way, we can soften the pain even a little.

Clasping Hands as a Source of Energy

When water was exposed to "clasping hands," it formed one of the crystals shown on page 49. Think for a moment about why people clasp their hands. No matter what the culture or religion, people clasp their hands together when asking something of the creator or of other people.

A ritual of the ancient Japanese religion of Shinto is to face the sun at about 4:30 in the morning, lifting up your arms and bringing your hands together as if you were absorbing the light into your soul. It is a way of gathering energy. By bringing the hands together, a simple form of energy from resonance forms and expands and enters your body.

Consider the character that the Japanese use to write "sound": 音. Pronounced *oto*, this character is actually formed of two simple characters, the top part meaning "to stand" and the bottom part meaning "sun." So it would seem that the people of long ago understood well the relationship between the vibration of sound and the sun.

Of course, modern science has now shown us that light is waves—vibration, if you will—and the source of our energy. And so it's not hard to imagine why people of ancient times faced the sun in the morning and asked to be a vessel of its energy by clasping their hands together.

The Power of Adoration

Is there someone for whom you feel adoration? If there's not, then I would like to encourage you to find such a person. Just looking at someone you adore has a purifying effect. Being around that person raises your spirits and causes you to sit just a little bit straighter.

The crystal influenced by the word "adoration" on page 49 is indicative of the love and respect that a child feels toward his or her parents, or the love and respect shared by an elderly couple.

The crystal influenced by the word "eternal," also on page 49, is formed around a distinctive hexagonal shape that appears as if it could go on forever. As I mentioned previously, if you consider that life is vibration, then it's not hard to understand how life can go on forever. The experience we know as death can define the extent of our physical life, but our vibration can go on resonating for eternity, regardless of what happens to flesh and bone.

The Power of Your Name

Write down your name and take a look at it—a really good look. Your name has the power for good or evil and the power to influence what road you choose in life. Now with a feeling of gratitude, take another look at your name, and you will then be able to feel something new—energy you've never felt before.

Not long ago in Japan, news was made by a father who tried to name his child "Devil." Although some argued that parents have the right to give their children any name they choose, the city refused to accept the name, and instead of taking it to court, the father backed down. When we exposed water to the word "devil," the result was the deformed crystal on page 83. By contrast, when water was exposed to the word "angel," the result was a beautiful formation of tiny crystals in a circle.

Japanese names are usually written with characters that express a trait the parents would like to instill in their children. Here is one of my favorite names: 真理. Pronounced *Mari*, this name means "truth." One of the crystals on page 83 was formed after being exposed to this name, and you can see the beautiful results.

The most common character in Japanese names is the character for "harmony": 和. This character, which formed the crystal on page 83, seems to form a circle, so perhaps it's more than a coincidence that this character is closely related to the word for "circle." Peace is often symbolized by a circle, and so this crystal with its complex formations seems to be telling us about the importance of peace in our troubled world.

Compliment Yourself for a Change

Compare the two crystals on page 85, which were formed after being exposed to "You're beautiful!" and "You're becoming beautiful." I have already mentioned the importance of complimenting yourself, but instead of complimenting yourself every day with the same words, try to find a new compliment for each new day. The effect will be slightly different each day as you evolve into a new person. New cells are continually being formed within our bodies, and by changing the words you praise yourself with, you can have a surprising amount of influence over how you change. It may be easier than you think to reset your life and become the person you truly want to be.

Next look at the crystal formed by "unhappiness" on page 88. Everyone knows people who are always complaining about how miserable their life is, but this crystal seems to be telling us just how destructive this word can be. Telling people how unhappy you are can bring little good, so instead let people know when you're happy.

Positive Words Come Back to You

Now let's look at the crystals formed by "You did well," "That's no good," "affection," and "hate" on pages 86 and 87. As you can clearly see, the photographs of the crystals influenced by "That's no good" and "hate" aren't pleasant to look at. What this shows is that the positive and negative images of words are clearly reflected in water. I'd like to encourage you to use words with positive images as often as possible. Positive words have the power to give positive vibrations to the people around you, and those same positive vibrations will eventually return to the source. Something similar can be said for negative words: After having a negative influence on those around you, the negative vibrations return to you to create a vicious cycle of negative vibration.

When you look at the crystal formed by "rage and murder" on page 87, perhaps you can imagine a masked person in hiding suddenly attacking an unsuspecting person. Some of the worst crystal formations that I've seen are those formed by words having to do with abuse and violence. Perhaps what we can learn from this is that when you seek to do harm or damage to others, you are at the same time inflicting similar harm or damage upon yourself.

Now consider the "Let's do it" and "Do it" crystals on page 89. While the "Let's do it" crystal is strikingly beautiful, the "Do it" crystal is somewhat similar to the crystal created by "devil." As I implied in an earlier chapter, the concept of "Do it" does not exist anywhere in nature. All we know about nature tells us that things happen naturally rather than being forced, and we would be doing ourselves a favor if we avoid using expressions such as "You have to" and "You'd better." A more attractive alternative is to value the true nature and spontaneity of yourself and others.

Sharing Your Feelings and Yourself

Everyone will agree that the crystal formed by the word "soul" on page 90 is indeed beautiful. The Japanese word for "soul," pronounced *tameshii*, is written in two parts, like this: 魂. The part on the left side looks like this: 云. This side of the character means "to speak," while the part on the right, taken alone, means "evil spirit." While it is said that silence is golden, keeping your feelings bottled up inside is certainly not recommended. In fact, it may be wise to be wary of people who refuse to share their feelings with you. I have found time and time again in my research of water crystals that the combination of crystal photographs and

Japanese characters gives surprising insight into the nature of words.

Making the Most of Positive Words

Consider the different crystals formed by the words "Thank you" and "I'm sorry" on page 92. The different formations are to be expected, considering that we use these two expressions in different circumstances. In the same respect, we choose the words we use depending on how we feel day by day and moment by moment.

As we go about our busy lives, how can we find the time to take advantage of the power of positive words? One possibility is to write or even tattoo good words on your body, but I, for one, have a hard time believing that tattoos are a positive thing. Instead of the body gaining power from the words written on it, I'm concerned that the body might actually become dependent on the power of such words. An old Japanese ghost story tells about a man who writes sutras all over his body to protect himself from devils. But he forgets to write sutras on his ears, so the devils bite them off, illustrating the fallible nature of writing on ourselves when we should be thinking about how we can incorporate these good words as part of our souls. Covering your body with the words *love* and *gratitude* is not nearly as effective as daily making the choice to go about your life with your heart filled with *love* and *gratitude*.

But instead of having only certain words as your constant mantra, I encourage you to consider, for each situation you face, what positive words would match. If you are experiencing something unpleasant, then you can think of a positive word or expression for that situation and focus that word or expression on the water within your body.

As we have seen, the expression "I'm sorry" creates quite a beautiful crystal. We can all think back to a situation where we should have used these words. If this is something you can relate to, I encourage you to look at the "I'm sorry" crystal, speak the offended person's name, and say, "I'm sorry."

The crystal on page 93 formed by the words "peace of mind" is stable and steady. It's not hard to feel peaceful vibrations from this lovely crystal. When you feel troubled or ill at ease, such as when you have an important interview or face a new

"Truth"

"Harmony"

The crystal formed by the word "truth" has a mysterious beauty. Albert Einstein said, "The most beautiful experience we can have is the mysterious." Harmony is all-encompassing, and a circle seems to be forming in this crystal when the word "harmony" is shown to it.

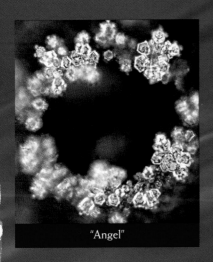

"Angel"

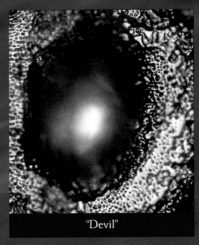

"Devil"

In contrast to the "devil" crystal, the "angel" crystal seems to be formed by an array of tiny crystals linked together.

"You're pretty" spoken repeatedly to water

"You're stupid" spoken repeatedly to water

Instead of exposing water to written stimulus, for these two crystals we repeated the expressions over and over. Spoken words seem to have the same effect as written words, which makes sense considering they both emit energy, or vibration.

"You're beautiful!"

"You're becoming beautiful."

We tried changing the words we used just a little. The result was a gradual change in the crystal, suggesting that we are reborn with each new day.

"You did well."

"That's no good."

The "You did well" crystal is indeed beautiful, while the "That's no good" crystal failed to form. By using positive words, you'll spread good vibrations to those around you, and those good vibrations will eventually return to you.

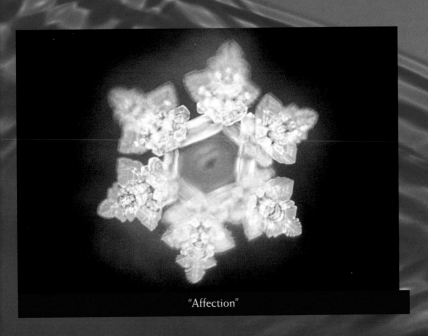

"Affection"

"Hate"

"Rage and murder"

While the "affection" crystal appears open and emerging, the "hate" crystal seems to be closed in. The formation from "rage and murder" ...es an image of someone hiding and waiting to attack.

87

"Happiness"

"Unhappiness"

"Happiness" resulted in a refined and highly detailed crystal. The second crystal makes it clear why "unhappiness" is a word that should be avoided.

"Let's do it."

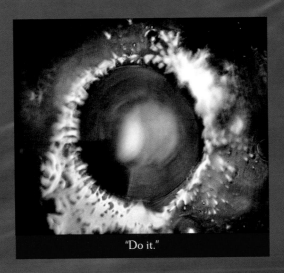

"Do it."

Here we have two vastly different crystals, reflecting the distinctly different energies of these two phrases.

"Soul"

"Evil spirit"

The Japanese character for "soul" is created by combining one character that means "to speak" with another that means "evil spirit," indicating the importance of expressing yourself precisely.

"Friend"

Water crystals formed by the word "friend" were extremely beautiful and reflected happiness. Moreover, when we look at the concept of "a circle of friends," we observe that when you make one friend, then, one by one, you make more friends.

"Thanks to you."

"The reason for living."

These phrases both created beautiful crystals, indicating that good words resonate and bring about positive results.

"Thank you."

"I'm sorry."

These two crystals indicate the importance of sincere gratitude and apology. If there is someone to whom you should apologize but have not, look at the "I'm sorry" crystal, say the offended person's name, and say, "I'm sorry." Apologizing within your heart is the next best thing to apologizing in person.

"Peace of mind"

This word created a beautiful and stable crystal. The Japanese character for "peace of mind" is represented by a woman beneath the roof of a home, indicating the role that women can have in creating a calm and stable environment.

"Self-love"

"Spousal love"

The crystal created by "self-love" is packed full of energy. Perhaps you can see hands raised in prayer in all directions. The "spousal love" crystal appears to be a smaller crystal protected by a larger one.

"Family love"

"Neighborly love"

The "family love" crystal appears to consist of three layers of water crystals, perhaps indicating grandparents, parents, and children. The "neighborly love" crystal seems to shine with harmony.

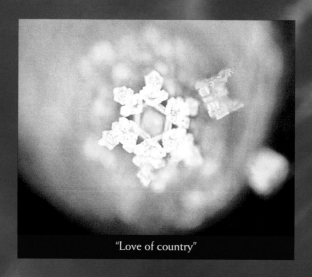

"Love of country"

"Love for humanity"

The "love of country" crystal seems to be supported by a larger crystal in the background. It is interesting that a small crown-shaped crystal formed off to the side. The "love for humanity" crystal is a beautiful geometrical formation.

Namu-amida-butsu chant

Namu-myoho-renge-kyo chant

Exposing water to Buddhist sutras resulted in the formation of beautiful crystals, explaining why writing and reading sutras has a soothing effect.

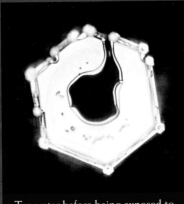

Tap water before being exposed to chanting

Tap water after being exposed to chanting

I placed samples of tap water on a stage where sixty Buddhist monks were chanting and recorded this remarkable change in crystal formations.

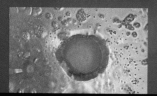

Water exposed to the electro-magnetic field of a mobile phone

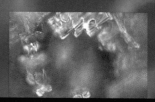

Water left sitting in front of a television for four hours

Water labeled "love and gratitude" exposed to the electromagnetic field of a mobile phone

Water labeled "love and gratitude" left sitting in front of a television

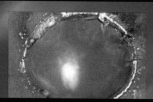

Water heated in a microwave oven

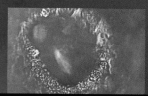

Water left sitting in front of a computer for four hours

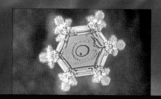

Water labeled "love and gratitude" heated in a microwave oven

Water labeled "love and gratitude" left sitting in front of a computer

All of the water exposed to electromagnetic fields received some damage, but the words "love and gratitude" counteracted some of the negative effects.

challenge, look at this photograph and let the peaceful vibration calm your soul.

The Soothing Vibration of Sutras

There are many ways to calm yourself; two popular ways are to keep a diary and to chant. That both of these activities relate to words is, I think, no coincidence. When we exposed two well-known Buddhist sutras to water, the result was the beautiful crystals on page 97. The sutras are known for a lovely chant-like vibration, and so this is the result we expected. It seems to me that the sutras form a conduit to the energy of the universe.

As you may know, there are seven chakras or "energy points" located along the body, from the top of the head and down through the spine, with each chakra having its own frequency. I believe that sutras, like the chakra at the top of the head, serve as portals for the energy of the universe. If you've ever heard the chanting of sutras, you'll know how simple and minimal the sounds are. But perhaps that is what makes them so powerful.

Recently in Japan, stage performances of sutra chants have been quietly gaining popularity. At one such performance by sixty monks, I placed some samples of water on the stage, resulting in the crystal formations on page 97. The soothing effects of these chants are evident in the pure, delicate crystals.

Loving Others Begins with Loving Yourself

The series of "love" photographs on pages 94 to 96 were very telling about the nature of love. In the "self-love" crystal, you can almost see hands clasped together as if in prayer in all four directions, forming what appears to be a high-energy crystal. This indicates just how important it is to love yourself for who you are. The concept of self-love is not easy to grasp, but think about it in terms of vibration and resonance: without your own positive vibration, you will be unable to help others vibrate. Simply put, it's impossible to love another unless you can first love yourself.

Let me give you an example of what I mean. Let's say that there's a 440-hertz tuning fork. If it's just standing there, there's not enough vibration to be audible by the human ear. But if you sing "Ah!" at this level the tuning fork will begin to vibrate. By sharing your vibration, you have restored the tuning fork—you have brought it back to life through an act of sharing. In this case, we might even say that the act of singing "Ah!" is a loving act.

Each one of us has an important responsibility to give love in the way that only a human can. Of course everything emits vibration, but not the continuous and conscious vibration that humans can. And we have another quality that makes us special: as human beings, we are capable of resonating with everything else in our world. We can resonate with all the sounds in the octave as well as with higher and even lower octaves. Perhaps you can't quite sing the *la* sound of a high octave, but you can resonate with that *la* using one from a lower octave. And this is why we are capable of resonating with and giving energy to anything and everything that is.

Neither the tree nor the flower is capable of independent vibration, but by speaking to a plant, you can breathe vibration and energy into its fibers. If you doubt this, just ask anyone who loves spending time with their plants. They'll tell you that they don't just take care of their plants, they speak to them. Understanding the principles of vibration and resonance may help give understanding to the unexplainable.

Capable of making all vibrations, the human being has a special place with the creator and has special powers to affect the world we live in. We have the power of thought and the power of free will, and thus the power to make whatever sound we desire, and in this we have the power to be a force for change.

But to give energy to the world around us, we must first have energy within us. You can't give someone something that you don't already have. So to have love in your life, begin by respecting, appreciating, and caring for yourself. When you feel secure in your self-love, then and only then will you be ready to share your love and your life with someone else. All successful unions begin with the love of your *self*—not with your love of someone else.

The Power to Make Others Happy

Now take a look at the "spousal love" crystal on page 94. The crystal appears to have two layers, with the smaller one encompassed by the larger one. This perhaps indicates that the secret of a good relationship is that the two are not the same: symbiosis does not require that one be dominant and the other subservient. The ability to reverse roles as needed is an indication of a healthy relationship, one upon which the love of family can be created.

The "family love" crystal on page 95 shows a group of three formations, perhaps indicative of grandparents, parents, and children living together in harmony. It's rather uncommon nowadays to find three generations living under one roof, but even if families live apart, they can still be of one heart. Grandma and grandpa don't need to be forgotten. If you take your children to see their grandparents, then your own children will probably do the same when you become the grandparent. The message from the crystal is that the family unit in its fullness—in the past, present, and future—is the combination of three.

When you have love for your family, then it is possible to love your neighbor. The "neighborly love" crystal on page 95 creates a beautiful image of harmony. And after you have become capable of love for your neighbor, you can next love your country.

The "love of country" crystal on page 96 looks as if it's sitting on a larger crystal in the background, indicating how our identity is closely related to the country of our origin. You can't help but feel sorry for the millions who have been forced by the dishevelment of these troubled times to give up their homeland. Perhaps the little crown off to the side on this crystal indicates that governance is required for countries to go on existing.

And then, after love of country, you are capable of love for humanity. The "love for humanity" crystal on page 96 seems to be an especially well-balanced and beautiful crystal. This is an important crystal because this type of love will help us solve the problems of war, famine, and worldwide disease.

These six crystals of love are all built on the love of self. If you'd like to have a part in spreading love to the world, then you must first love yourself deeply and completely. Some people might think that they already focus too much on their own needs, but that's actually a good starting point. You will soon realize that having self-love is not being self-centered. Self-love is the energy required for loving another person, your family, your neighbor, your country, and all your fellow human beings.

Moving toward Peace

As I mentioned previously, water that was shown the characters for "peace" formed crystals in a shape that looked like the joined crystals formed when water was shown the words "love and gratitude" (see page 35). I feel this means that when "love" harmonizes with "gratitude," you get "peace."

If thoughts of peace are not coming into your heart, you should recall love and gratitude, especially the latter. Being thankful brings you love; being thankful even helps create love within your being. When you heap love on top of thanks, your soul will be at peace.

Peace must be created first by individuals. In this way, peace will spread to your family. This sense of peace, in turn, evolves into love that permeates a region, an entire nation, and finally the entire world. It is you, yourself, who becomes peace. In order to accomplish this you need to pile thanks on top of love.

I believe that our planet is sick. When people take ill, the weakest parts of their body develop symptoms of illness. People who experience weakness in their throat often eventually develop a disease in their throat. The same holds true for other organs of the body. People with weak lungs are prone to developing a lung disease just as people with a weak stomach are more likely to develop a stomach condition.

Our planet works in much the same way. Earth is like a diseased patient who is sorely in need of medical assistance. For example, look at Afghanistan, Iraq, Israel, the Indian Ocean, Pakistan, Thailand, and Mexico's Yucatan Peninsula. In all of these places, disastrous conditions in the form of wars, earthquakes, tidal waves, and hurricanes are occurring. It is as if the planet's immune system is weak and losing cellular matter as a result.

Why are these things happening? One by one, the earth's harmony is being seriously tampered with. Only through the phenomenon of resonance are the vibrations of energy's essence able to give us beautiful, peaceful energy.

At this time, "harmony" and "peace" are missing in our world. As long as we continue destroying "harmony," the planet is going to experience more and more natural disasters and war. As for us residents of this planet, make no mistake that the conditions of life are going to become tougher and tougher unless we do something to reverse the course.

I am Japanese and must never forget the ancient spirit of my native land, originally called Yamato before it became known as Japan. The Japanese word for "harmony," 和 (pronounced "wa"), makes up half of the Japanese word for "peace, 平和 (pronounced "heiwa"). This character 和 ("harmony") is also seen regularly as part of the ancient word for Japan, 大和 "great harmony" (usually pronounced "Yamato"). In daily Japanese, "harmony" 和, is widely used to represent "Japan" or "Japanese" (food, language, style, architecture and the like). In all these ways, the symbol for "harmony," 和, permeates Japanese life. I feel that it is my task to dispatch this message to the world: "Get back in harmony." The starting point for this endeavor is to create harmony. Bring harmony back to your marriage, bring harmony to your family, and bring harmony to the people in your neighborhood. With this kind of thinking, we can create the foundation for a world that is more and more harmonious.

It is difficult to create world peace by yourself. And yet, by creating harmony within the lives of individuals a broader, more profound harmony will develop, step by step, in our world. When this kind of thinking comes naturally to you, you will be able to make a large contribution to peace.

Living with Clean Water:
Finding Peace and Comfort

Energy Giving Energy

Living life to its fullest requires a considerable degree of positive energy, and to harbor this positive energy within yourself requires resonation. The resonance that I refer to comes from aligning yourself with the resonance of love and gratitude while also emitting vibrations of love and gratitude.

That is easily said, but how do we actually make it a part of who we are and what we do? In this chapter, we'll look at some of the specific ways that you can live life within this positive energy without being distracted by the negative stress that so easily besets us.

I have already mentioned that to vibrate in a positive way requires that you resonate with someone else's positive vibrations. Resonance is what we use to share our energy with each other. In the same way, when we align our words and thoughts to the grand principles of nature and the will of the creator, we can experience positive vibration and happiness. This energy makes us feel alive and full of energy. But when we are out of alignment with this energy, we soon feel stressed and depressed. Of course, the foundation for the grand principles of the universe and the will of the creator is nothing less than love and gratitude.

By giving vibration—energy—to those around us, we give them love. This, the intentional sharing of the energy of love is something that all human beings are uniquely capable of. Positive words have the power to give energy to the receiver while also having the same effect on the giver.

When a person is loved, the natural result is gratitude, and when gratitude and love exist together in the same sphere, the natural result is resonance. When a sick child is nursed back to health by the love of his or her parents, feelings of gratitude result. And then when the roles are reversed, the child, out of gratitude, cares for the parents with love, as the loving giver becomes the grateful receiver.

The Difference between Negative and Positive People

We are all capable of emitting beautiful healing vibrations. These are the vibrations that loving mothers and fathers send to their children.

As I have mentioned before, water, as the ultimate transmitter, is capable of capturing and relaying anything and everything. So if there's something that's not right about the water within your body, you will be unable to receive the positive vibrations that surround you. If the container of water is deformed, the vibration will also be deformed.

A negative person hears positive words as negative. Perhaps you know someone like that. We can easily surmise that the very structure of the water of such a deformed thinker is also deformed. Such people are incapable of enjoying what is right and good about the world, and they have an enormous capacity for creating a dark cloud on the most positive of happenings, serving as an illustration of the importance of good water.

When people have caved in to the stresses of society and daily life, their vibration becomes distorted, and even the kindest of words will have little or no effect on them. When you've reached that point, it becomes difficult to improve the water within yourself on your own. But if you open your eyes, you'll realize that there are people all around you who are able and willing to share their positive energy with you. If you are able to share your love, then I hope you will be willing to do so. Love is one thing you never have to worry about running out of.

When you have made it a habit to extend a loving hand to those around you, whenever you find yourself down and discouraged, loving hands will raise you up.

The Same Wavelength

Think about when you last picked up a little baby. Did you find yourself speaking in a soft, gentle voice? No matter what language you speak or what culture you're from, we all speak to babies in the same way. The reason, simply put, is because we are aligning ourselves with the vibrations of the baby. We all subconsciously understand that a baby's vibration is short, resulting in the soft sounds that all babies make, and when we align ourselves with this vibration, we make similar sounds.

Perhaps you have also realized that your voice and manner of speaking change depending on whom you talk to. When I talk to someone, I intentionally try to speak in a way that will put me in harmony with that person. But even the vibrations of any one person will change depending on the mood of the moment, as revealed by the speed and pitch of the voice.

I suspect that you have experienced times when your vibration has been in harmony with someone else's. You might have come away from such an experience saying, "We just seemed to resonate." This is something that we do at an instinctive level, so unless you think about it, you might not even be aware that it's happening.

When you align your voice with the vibration of the other person, you can choose what note on the scale you are going to use. If you wish to comfort a friend suffering from a broken heart, are you going to choose *do-mi-so* or *do-fa-la*? You might say, "Heartbreak opens the doors for something new," or maybe, "Better things await you." But whatever you say, you'll speak it in gentle, loving tones.

When you talk to a person in distress, they may vibrate in all the possible notes on the musical scale, but you can use kind and loving words to create the opposing notes to offset the negativity. Perhaps the highest compliment you can pay to someone is to say that they have the ability to see things from another's position. Such people are capable of listening, showing they understand, and then saying the words that make the other person realize that it's not the end of the world. That's what resonating with another means.

If you know someone who seems cold and uncaring, consider that they may just be poor at putting themselves in the position of others and aligning themselves with others' vibrations. You may have sought comfort from such a person only to come away feeling worse than ever. It's simply impossible to comfort others if you can't feel their feelings and align yourself with their vibration.

A Beauty Treatment That Requires Neither Time nor Money

To feel something that stirs your emotions each day is the way to find the energy for a full and rewarding life.

Emotion is motion, which makes it no coincidence that the phenomenon of resonance is the combination of emotion and movement. By resonating with someone, we experience powerful vibration—powerful energy, if you will. And the deeper the emotion, the more clear and pure are the vibrations that we experience.

I often give lectures, and when those lectures go well, I know that there was resonance between myself and the audience, that I have in some way stirred their emotions. I've stirred emotions when what I have said has entered the listener's mind as energy and memory. It happens when the way I see the world becomes the way another person sees the world.

The level of enjoyment, vitality, and meaning of each day is directly related to the degree that we allow our emotions to be stirred by what goes on around us.

Shizue Kato, a well-known women's rights activist, was asked by a newspaper reporter on her hundredth birthday what her secret to longevity was. "Get excited about something at least ten times a day," she replied. "It's exciting to wake up in the morning and realize you're still alive and breathing. It's exciting to have something really delicious for breakfast. It's exciting to see a beautiful morning glory blooming outside. You can get emotional about the charity of the warm sunshine and the blessings of the falling rain. If you just take the time to look around and see even the most insignificant of things, you'll realize that the world is full of things to get emotional about." These are words to live by, indeed.

For Better-Tasting Water

We want to purify the water within our bodies, but we also want to make the water that we drink as pure as possible. Here's an easy way to do that: before you take a drink of water, pause a moment and look at it. With warm, benevolent feelings, say "Thank you" to the water, and then drink it. I do this throughout the day, whenever I take a drink of water, and it makes a noticeable difference.

As I've mentioned previously, vocalizing words strengthens the vibration, so saying "Thank you" to water before drinking it results in a change in water's taste. The moment you say "Thank you," the positive vibration needed for beautiful crystals begins. The vibration spreads to the water in the atmosphere, forming an expanding ring of vibration that your body feels. Water is water, whether it's in a cup, in the atmosphere, or in your body; they are fundamentally linked. The water outside of you resonates with the water within you.

Daily Fulfillment through Water

Ask yourself how conscious you are of water as you go about your daily life. If you're like most people, you probably don't consider it much. I'd like to give you a few suggestions for making water a conscious part of your life.

First, when you wake up in the morning, take a cup that is labeled with the words "Love and gratitude" and fill it with water. Then, with reverence in your heart, drink the water. After drinking the water, face the sun. The sun is a source of special energy. Just as the ancients of Japan did in the earliest days of Shinto spiritualism, place your hands together and face the sun so as to take in its energy. I also recommend placing your hands together in gratitude before you eat.

Morning is a hectic time for most of us, but I encourage you to make your mornings more relaxing and leisurely. Take time to enjoy the flowers along the way. A Japanese saying goes that if one of the tea leaves in your morning tea stands upright in your cup, you'll have good luck that day. But maybe the luck will come to the one who takes the time to consider the leaves in the teacup. If you think having a hectic morning is a natural way to start the day, try getting up thirty minutes earlier—not to do more but to do less.

To make your morning more relaxing, think of nature right when you wake up. Greet your pet if you have one or water a plant and say something to it. ("I love you" is always a good choice of words.) When you make a habit of this, the plant will grow to be strong and healthy. But often when we become ill and are unable to give a plant positive energy, the plant will dry up and die—that's how important the phenomenon of resonation is. Learning to slow down and take your time in the morning will reveal to you the strength of this power.

Now for your evening routine: taking a long, hot bath can be a good way to relax your body and mind after a stressful day. Close your eyes and feel the vibration of water all over your body. Fill your soul with appreciation for the water. The ideal temperature for bathwater is around 104 to 107 degrees Fahrenheit. Heat is a result of vibration, and so covering your body in water of this temperature can be extremely comforting, helping you to expel fatigue and negative vibrations.

Hot springs throughout the world are desired for their ability to aid in relaxation, and one of the things that make them so enjoyable is the vibrational effect of the water. The vibration enters your body and pushes out the negative vibration, resulting in the formation of a healthy and vibrant metabolism.

There's so much that water does for us: it warms our bodies, replenishes the dry parched throat, and carries away our waste without ever a complaint. When you think about all the things that water does for us, how can you not help but be filled with gratitude?

It shouldn't be a stretch of the imagination to understand why taking a nice, warm bath can feel akin to what a baby feels like when cradled in its mother's arms. If you begin to see the water in your bathtub as amniotic fluid, it can make the experience all the more relaxing.

At home in your own bath, you might try various bath salts. And if there's a baby in the house, I recommend writing the words "love and gratitude" on the baby's toy. After your bath and before you go to bed, take a drink of love and gratitude in the form of water. Then place your hands together in thanks for your pets, your plants, and your loved ones.

Perhaps you have your own routine for relaxing at night, but I like to listen to relaxing music as I drift off to sleep. This, I believe, helps the water within me return to its pristine, beautiful origin as the stress of the day leaves my body. Near your bed, have access to different types of music—classical, jazz, anything—to help you relax from the particular stresses of the day.

Avoiding Stress-Induced Illnesses

Too much stress leads to illness, which is why you should aim to make every morning and evening relaxing. Stress arises when the vibration that you should be experiencing becomes deformed. Deformed vibration builds up, and the result is ultimately and inevitably illness.

A great variety of vibrations exist within our bodies, and the stresses of daily life often change them slowly and gradually. When the change first begins at the subatomic level, there are no outward signs, but as the change reaches the molecular and cellular levels, symptoms begin to appear. If the stress continues, then the change in vibration will move from the cells to the organs, health will deteriorate, and death will loom. The messenger that carries this deterioration is, of course, water.

As mentioned, vibration is maintained by the phenomenon of resonance. There is nothing stronger or purer than the resonance of two positive vibrations. You can stay healthy and happy by freeing yourself from stress and finding pure resonance created by pure vibration. You can do this by taking time for any activity that helps you forget your troubles and experience moments of quiet peace. Finding moments of peace helps you put your life back together, consciously purify the water within you, and begin to live the life you want to live.

Use the energy you get when talking to a friend to neutralize negative vibrations, or enjoy a massage or some other relaxation technique to calm yourself and get back on your feet. Taking a bus or train ride can help you relax, too. Let the rumbling of the journey rock and lull you—it might be just the vibration you've been looking for. You might want to do some experimenting to find a type of music that helps you relax. Water will hear the music and be purified by its positive effects.

The Nature of Electromagnetic Fields
I mentioned in a previous chapter the danger of too much exposure to electromagnetic fields. (See

page 98 for photographs of water exposed to various electromagnetic fields.) While we do not need to throw away our cell phones and become obsessed with avoiding electromagnetic fields, it's important that we keep our words and thoughts centered around love and gratitude.

We can't live without cell phones, microwave ovens, televisions, and computers; living with electromagnetic fields just seems to come with the territory. Almost every little thing we do in this modern world seems to require the generation of electromagnetic fields. Understanding their nature will help you get electromagnetic fields to work for you. And that involves making love and gratitude a part of everything you think and do.

It's not essential that you unplug the television, but you can choose to watch only good and wholesome programs. Your computer is fine where it's at, just as long as you use it as a positive tool. Go ahead and use your cell phone, but don't use it to carry on negative or angry conversations.

How about your microwave oven? This device uses microwaves to vibrate the atoms of the food at a rapid enough rate to cause the food to heat up, and to assume that this has an effect on your nervous system requires no great leap of logic. Microwaves are of course designed so as to have only a minimal effect on us, but the water within the heated food has recorded the effect of the microwaves, and you can't help but wonder if it is the best thing to consume.

If you would rather not get rid of your microwave, then I suggest that you use your microwave with love and gratitude. The best thing you can do is to say "I love you" to the food as it heats up; another, less proactive, measure is to simply place "love and gratitude" stickers on the microwave containers.

Likewise, we need to be conscious of the way we use the Internet. You may be surprised to learn that the words you write in e-mails and text messages have a stronger effect on your body than the words you use in conversations and letters. This is because the vibration of the human nervous system is actually on the same level as the vibration of electronic communication systems such as e-mail and chatrooms. When you write something by hand or print something, the vibration is not fine enough to resonate with your nervous system, limiting the effect that the vibration can have on you. But writing involving electronic fields harmonizes perfectly with the vibration of your nervous system, resulting in the formation of resonance and making it possible for an e-mail or text message to have an enormous effect on your brain and body.

Words carried on electronic waves have the power to go right to the core of the receiver, having a devastating and lasting effect. By contrast, sending warm words of praise can have a positive effect on the well-being of the receiver. If you have something negative to say about someone, e-mail is not the place to do it. Companies are used to getting complaints from clients through e-mail, and many people have received a rebuke from a superior in the form of a text message, but if you wish to limit the harm caused by your negative vibrations, then reserving these kinds of messages for face-to-face meetings is always a good idea. If you feel it's easier to express your true feelings through e-communication, then try to express yourself with positive and encouraging messages.

Voice communication via cell phone also deserves attention. Unlike the old telephones connected by cable, cell phones use electronic fields, and thus they, too, are a matter of concern. Positive conversations on your cell phone are one thing, but when the discussion turns dark, the danger can range from anything from a harmed relationship to serious physical damage.

Normal words spoken face-to-face with no particular harmful effect can become a damaging weapon through a cell phone. The potential damage of harsh and hateful words communicated by cell phone should be enough to make us all careful about the words we use when we talk on these devices. It is but one more reason to try to keep your thoughts and words positive at all times.

Freedom from Negative Emotions

When you think about negative emotions in light of what we know about vibration, it isn't hard to realize how and why irritation, frustration, and envy can be detrimental to your health. Anger and excitement raise the rate of vibration in your body and lead to an abnormal physical condition. Anger, for example, can be especially hard on your liver. In Eastern medicine, the close relationship between the emotion of anger and the liver has been accepted as common knowledge for centuries; it is well known that anger will destroy the cells of the liver, explaining why people suffering from cirrhosis and hepatitis tend to have hot tempers.

Sadness can be harmful to the cells of the hippocampus in the brain, increasing the risk of Alzheimer's. Sadness can also affect the blood and lead to leukemia and other blood-related illnesses. Envy can damage the thyroid gland.

Why an emotion can have an effect on a particular organ of the body can be explained by the differing wavelengths caused by each emotion. Day in and day out, our emotions vibrate the atoms and molecules within our bodies. It may be hard to avoid all negative emotions, but with love and gratitude you do have the ability to neutralize all the negative emotions you may experience. When you feel the onset of a negative emotion, then in your mind, just imagine the opposite emotion.

If, for example, you feel pangs of resentment and you don't want that emotion to harm your health, take refuge in the emotion of gratitude, the opposite of resentment. Gratitude can neutralize resentment because they are both on the same wavelength—on the negative side is resentment, and on the positive side is gratitude. But if someone has resentment for you, then responding to that person with gratitude requires the fiber and fortitude that most of us don't have. When in the heat of such a situation, I suggest that you form an image of someone for whom you do feel gratitude. When you get a call from someone who can make your blood boil, think of the pleasant face of someone you know, and soon you'll free yourself from the negative feelings and be able to fill your heart with gratitude.

Keep the recommendations of this chapter in mind and you will be well on your way to making water a conscious part of every day.

Love and Gratitude and
Saving the World

Free Energy: One Measure of Love and Two Measures of Gratitude

Let me explain how we can improve the water outside our bodies through the power of crystals of love and gratitude. As I mentioned previously, the act of improving the water within our bodies is at the same time the act of improving the water that covers our planet. So once you love and appreciate the water inside yourself, you can help improve the water of the world.

When we consider water atoms, then we can easily see the role that water plays on our planet. Water has two hydrogen atoms and one oxygen atom, in other words, H_2O. Whenever I consider this chemical formula for water, I cannot help butthink of the relationship between love and gratitude, with love being oxygen and gratitude being hydrogen.

There can be no flame without oxygen, and without flame there can be no heat. And without oxygen, life would come to a quick end. So without love, or oxygen, the continuation of life would not be possible. When on the receiving end of love, an extra dose of gratitude is always appropriate. In response to one part love, two parts gratitude forms the balance of life.

When it comes to energy, the structure of one part love and two parts gratitude creates a type of *free energy*. Let me explain: Let's say that I try to tell something to someone. If the other person resonates or gains an understanding of what I'm trying to say, then his or her heart will be stirred and the person will begin to vibrate. And when that happens, they will be open to receiving love at a deep level. The vibration from that person will spread to others, as the receiver of the vibration of love becomes the giver of the vibration of love. Another way of saying this is that one part love becomes two parts of vibration, and this is the basic concept of vibration.

But that is not the end of free energy. Free energy spreads out and the vibration goes on and on. I recently had an interesting experience that illustrates this. On February 6, 2005, I started a lecture tour that would take me from Santa Monica, California, to Hawaii. Two days before the first seminar, only about half of the tickets had been sold, but on the day of the seminar, the tickets started to sell. We soon realized that many more people wanted to come than what we had planned on. What caused this? It was the energy of a few individuals widening and spreading to others. The result was a sold-out event, with many in the audience experiencing love and gratitude when it had been initiated by just a handful.

Water as a Divine Messenger

As we already know, water responds with beautiful crystals when we expose it to positive words, and the opposite is true as well, but let's take a closer look at the mechanism from a different perspective.

To understand the complex nature of the existence of our universe and our own existence in that universe, we need a model in order to make any progress. My model consists of four parts: the creator (vibration), water (messenger), crystals (blueprint), and phenomena (matter and physical bodies).

Water crystals can be described as little blueprints for the design of our world. We can also make the assumption that when the creator set about to create this universe, the first project was the creation of water—the messenger, if you will, needed to deliver the architect's intention. The next question is, what is intention? I like to think that it is love and gratitude. I believe that before the universe was created, there was first a concept, a prelude to conception that could be described as the concept of love and gratitude. And perhaps this is why these two words create crystals more beautiful than any others.

Now let's look at the role water plays in the delivery of this intention. The ancient Greek philosopher Thales said that water is the basic building block of all matter. It's hard to disagree with this, but I'd like to express this concept in a slightly different way, while risking the possibility that some might find my description a little too religious for their tastes.

Of all of the creator's creations, water is unique. It is a type of conductor that can link the various dimensions of creation. Extending this metaphor, we can say that half of the body is in this third-dimensional world, and half is in a higher-level dimension.

The creator, also being in a higher dimension, is a being of matter and light that vibrates at an inconceivably fast rate. And when you think about it in that way, it shouldn't be hard to consider this divine being as the Sun or the Light of our world who created this world in order for us to have a place where we would be able to grow and develop to prepare for a higher dimension.

The creator saw that a physical body would facilitate the process of growth and development, and so water, entrusted with divine intention, was sent down, and it materialized into the first crystal. And then another crystal was formed, and then another, until intention formed life in all the diversity we know today. So Thales did get it right when he said that all comes from water, but perhaps I like to say that water is the messenger of the intention from the source of all existence. Understanding this helps you see how words can affect the formation of water.

When we show a word to the water—the divine messenger—if the word is a word of the divine, then the water will respond with a "yes," or beautiful, crystal, and if it is not, the response is a "no," or deformed, crystal.

However, in the last few decades, we have been facing a serious problem that threatens the underpinnings of the model I have described. The speed at which technology has developed in recent years has had results that are negative and against the natural and divine laws given to us. Harmful and destructive words, the harmonizing with electronic devices, and our disassociation with nature all threaten to disrupt the balance needed to maintain our planet and our existence on it. The corruption of words has become the corruption of country, the corruption of our planet, and perhaps worst of all, the corruption of our souls.

Stemming the Tide of Negativity

If love and gratitude retreat from the world, they will be replaced by negative vibration. In this age, the weakening of love and gratitude in one part of the world can become the cause for wars and disasters on the other side of the planet.

The decline of love and gratitude takes place in war zones like the Middle East, but it reaches beyond the battlefield and makes the I'm-the-only-one-who-matters belief the norm of our age. The decay within the soul seeps out to disrupt the world in ways we can hardly imagine or understand. And water, the mirror of the soul, the messenger of the creator, feels this and knows all, and this includes the imbalance that prevails all around us.

Water forms the world we live in and the universe the world exists in, creating a cosmic soup, if you will. Air, atmosphere, and light are all water in one form or another, but water all the same. Starting from the outer core of our planet to the very center, each layer contains water in either large or small amounts, and that, pretty much alone, is what accounts for their differences.

Since water permeates our entire planet and everything on it, the water of the world cannot help but reflect the decline that takes place within a human soul, as revealed by the formation of beautiful crystals and not-so-beautiful crystals.

The people who lived on earth for millions of years in a balanced relationship with water now worship power, profit, and self-interest. And none of this goes on without being noticed by water. The natural disasters in the world may actually be a little less natural and a little more man-made than we care to think. I realize that convincing a geologist of the relationship between what goes on in your heart and what goes on under the ground is no easy task, but that doesn't stop me from believing that the natural disasters of our age may be nothing more than the buildup of pressure within your heart rather than between continental plates.

Human Consciousness and Disasters

You don't have to go back far in history to find a time when the human population on the planet was much smaller than it is now. On the first day of the Christian era (1 A.D.), the population is estimated to have been about 200 million people, and the figure rose gradually and steadily until 1900, when it reached 1.5 billion. And then from 1900 to 2000, the population exploded, reaching and exceeding 6 billion.

When people were still rare on the planet, the effect of the consciousness of a single person on the water of the earth was probably insignificant, but as the population expanded, perhaps starting from around 1850 when the population exceeded a billion, the negative and evil consciousness of humankind began to be reflected in natural disasters around the planet. Now, with the population exceeding 6.5 billion, perhaps we should not be so surprised by all the fighting and wars going on around us. If 6.5 billion people continue to think the way they do now, we'll be lucky if the planet lasts another twenty years.

The risks our planet faces are not only of the sudden kind. The environment of our planet is moving closer to a planet-wide crisis that is fast approaching the point of no return.

Heat is vibration. You probably already know that heat results when atoms vibrate, and that explains how a microwave oven is able to create a sudden burst of heat. What will happen as the temperature of the planet increases at the current rate? After the temperature rises an average of 2 degrees centigrade, life will still be sustainable, but if it goes up two more degrees, then the earth will no longer be able to provide the environment and food necessary to sustain human life.

It's said that the planet's temperature has already risen 2 degrees in the last hundred years, causing massive melting at the North and South Poles, and it's now expected that the temperature will rise three degrees in the coming one hundred years.

Think about your own body temperature, especially how you feel when you have a fever. There's not an exact parallel between the planet and the human body, but if the planet's temperature does rise as expected, then we will all be living on a very sick planet indeed.

Ourselves and our planet both require stable vibration in order to survive. The vibration that compensates for a loss of love and gratitude can come in the form of a pistol, a bomb, or perhaps terrorism—all negative and abnormal vibration used to rule the world. The war in the Middle East and all the other wars going on around the planet are excessive vibration, leading to the acceleration of the burning up of our planet. It is also the mechanism for the disruption of the water that covers our planet, leading to earthquakes, tsunami, floods, typhoons, hurricanes, and droughts.

The Process of Self-Realization

Despite the negative outlook we're faced with, all hope is not yet lost. There are things we can do even now. We just have to follow the example of the natural world.

In the microscopic world, 10 percent of the microbes are generally considered bad, and 10 percent are considered good. The remaining 80 percent are neutral. This might have parallels in our own world. The battle for the survival of our planet is between the 10 percent working to destroy it and the 10 percent working to save it. When the 10 percent making up the good population win, then the neutral 80 percent will join them, and so that's why there is still hope. It is this

10 percent of the population that I hope to reach with my message of love and gratitude.

And here's why I think we can win: When the same number of good and bad microbes come together, the good microbes win.

This perspective is also supported by an experiment with water crystals.

When we put two labels—one saying "Thank you" and one saying "You fool!"—on water samples, the result was always the beautiful gratitude crystals. So if ten out of every one hundred people in the world open their eyes to love and gratitude, the planet can be saved.

The earth is the way it is because that is the way the creator made it. It and all the living creatures on it are designed with the ability to return to the point where all is well and right. Every life has a degree of pain and suffering, but there is nothing that is too negative to teach us something.

No matter who you are, there'll never be a shortage of people who come along to ruin your perfect day. That can either bring you down, or it can provide you with an opportunity to learn from responding with love and gratitude. And after you've learned all you need to learn, then you will be ready to graduate from this school of tribulation. And that is what life on earth is.

At three separate times, three different people with spiritual powers have told me that I've been reborn 700 times on this planet. This is nothing to brag about when you consider that it might mean I've failed to graduate 700 times. I'm now attempting to live my life to its fullest so I don't have to wait another lifetime to go to the next level beyond. I try my best to keep love and gratitude in my heart and to share positive vibration with those around me. I hope that you have been inspired by this book and will join me.

~~~~~~~~~~~~~~~~~~~~~~

Water and the Expanding
Circle of Peace

O n May 26, 2005, I gave a lecture on the energy of love and gratitude at the United Nations in New York City. The lecture was part of a twelve-part seminar based on themes related to spiritualism, the first of its kind ever for the United Nations.

This opportunity came to me by way of Ida Urso of Italy, who chaired the Spiritual Dimensions of Science and Consciousness Subcommittee of the NGO Committee on Spirituality, Values and Global Concerns. Ida had read and resonated with my book *The Hidden Messages in Water*. When she asked me to give a lecture, she said, and I'm paraphrasing, "The way the United Nations and the NGO see the world plays an important role in achieving the UN goals, but there will be very few people in the audience who realize that. As long as we are attached to outdated paradigms, we will never be able to find new solutions. To achieve our goals and to move humankind from a culture of war to a culture of peace, we need to promote the importance of spirituality—the importance of love and kindness. We would like Dr. Emoto to speak on the energy of compassion formed by one part of love and two parts of gratitude."

Of course I accepted her invitation and was able to make considerable progress in showing some of the most important people and greatest thinkers in the world how to create free energy combining one part love and two parts gratitude. The experience reminded me that without a fundamental change in our paradigm, we will never overcome the many serious challenges that we face in our day. It also convinced me that this combination of love and gratitude, a product of twenty years of research and experience into water and vibration, could be used as the yardstick for the creation of a new paradigm and new values throughout the world.

Had it not been for the publication of my books, I would have not been nearly as far down the road on my journey as I am now. The books led to a lecturing tour starting in March 2000 that has made it possible for me to reach even more people around the globe. In this book, I have tried to include the information that people have resonated with the most in lectures given in over three hundred cities over the last six years. I hope it will serve as a kind of primer to help more and more people understand the function and importance of vibration.

I encourage you to frequently revisit the crystal photographs and reread just a section a day. Imagine beautiful words and recall the beautiful crystals created by these words. That's enough. Just love and gratitude. And if you never forget this as you go about your daily life, your life will be one of happiness and joy.